THE U.N. BUILDING

THE U.N. BUILDING

Foreword by Kofi A. Annan
Essay by Aaron Betsky

Photographs by Ben Murphy

With 150 illustrations, 125 in color

Thames & Hudson

Acknowledgments
A number of U.N. staff provided valuable information.
The Publisher wishes to thank everyone, and, in particular,
the U.N. Archives and Photo Library, the Architects, the
Security Guards, and the Guided Tours Unit.

Ben Murphy would like to thank Kofi A. Annan, Casa Vogue,
everyone in Dpiros Badget, Lucas Dietrich, Carlo Ducci, Fred
Eckhard, Hugo Guinness, Renata Morteo, Edward Mortimer,
Damon Murray, Dominic Rushe, Howard Sooley, Stephen Sorrell,
Christopher Woodthorpe, Lucy Zannetti.

First published in 2005 in hardcover in the United States of America
by Thames & Hudson Inc., 500 Fifth Avenue,
New York, New York 10110

thamesandhudsonusa.com

Library of Congress Catalog Card Number 2005923454

ISBN-13: 978-0-500-34216-9
ISBN-10: 0-500-34216-4

Design by Murray & Sorrell FUEL

Printed and bound in Hong Kong by Sing Cheong Printing Co. Ltd.

Quotations
40 *The New York Times Magazine*, 20 April 1947.
44 From a U.N. hand-out titled "The United Nations: Some Basic
     Concepts," p. 5.
52 "GA Assembly" in *Architectural Forum*, October 1952; cited in
     Robert A. M. Stern, Thomas Mellins, David Fishman, *New York
     1960: Architecture and Urbanism Between the Second World
     War and the Bicentennial* (New York: The Monacelli Press, 1995),
     p. 625.
54 From Kofi A. Annan's address to the General Assembly in
     December 1996, after having been appointed seventh
     Secretary-General.
62 Rem Koolhaas and Bruce Mau, *S,M,L,XL* (New York: The
     Monacelli Press, 1995), p. 363.
91 Le Corbusier, "Declaration", 18 April 1947 in George A. Dudley,
     *A Workshop of Peace: Designing the United Nations Headquar-
     ters* (New York: The Architectural History Foundation, 1994),
     p. 213; partially cited in Adam Bartos and Christopher Hitchens,
     International Territory (New York: Verso, 1994), p. 17.
118 Lewis Mumford, "The Sky Line: Magic with Mirrors – 1,"
     New Yorker, 15 September 1951; cited in *New York 1960*, p. 619.
120 Trygve Lie to Dag Hammarskjöld, 9 April 1953; cited on
     www.un.org.
142 "The United Nations: Some Basic Concepts", p. 2.
157 *New York Post*, 6 January 1947.

Jacket (back): "The Sky Line: Magic with Mirrors – 1"; cited in
     New York 1960, p. 618.

Picture Credits
United Nations/Fuller-Turner-Walsh-Slattery Photo: 8, 11,
     17 (above), 19
United Nations: 13, 15, 17 (above), 18, 20, 21, 23, 24, 26, 27, 29

Contents

Foreword

KOFI A. ANNAN
Secretary-General

I will always recall my first impressions of the United Nations Building—its light, its space, its harmony. This book opens our doors to many new visitors, leading them on an illustrated journey through the complex. It captures the beauty of the spaces, and provides insights into the building's current functions. With each page, we see how what began as a vision of Trygve Lie, the first Secretary-General, to "develop the most beautiful and most efficient group of buildings in the world," grew into a recognized classic of modern architecture.

The book comes at a time of renewal for the Organization. While it marks our sixtieth anniversary, 2005 is also a year in which we are thinking *ahead*, and engaging in a constructive debate about the future: how to defeat poverty; how to build a collective security system able to meet our common threats; how to increase respect for human rights in every land; and how to adapt the United Nations to the needs and challenges of the 21st century. At the same time, we need to renovate and reinvigorate the building in which we work. Not only does much of the infrastructure require upgrading, the space itself needs to better accommodate the demands of the new century. It is reassuring to know that while the Capital Master Plan renovations move ahead, the pages of *The U.N. Building* will remain open, even if some of our doors are closed temporarily.

Sixty years ago, the immediate challenge was more practical than substantial: giving the newly founded world body, which at the time comprised only 51 Member States, an appropriate permanent home in the United States—the host country designated by the General Assembly—and selecting the design that would best symbolize its world headquarters. After a lively public debate, both the Manhattan location and a resolutely modern, collegial architecture project were chosen and supported by the then Secretary-General as well as by other U.N. officials, Member States delegates, and federal authorities.

Today, the membership of the United Nations stands at 191 States. More than 38 million visitors have toured the U.N. Building since its opening in the early 1950s. Countless thousands have called it their workplace. All of them have their own memories and impressions. As diverse as these may be, I am sure they recall the U.N. Building as a source of inspiration. Surely no greater tribute can be paid to a place that is home to the world.

New York, 2005

The General Assembly Hall under construction

Staging the Future: The U.N. Building as Symbol of a New World

AARON BETSKY

A Beautiful Symbol of Bureaucracy

The U.N. Building is a poem of bureaucracy in glass and stone. In it, the managerial revolution that finally rid the world of the last vestiges of outmoded forms of government has found a home, a headquarters and a workshop. If today neither managers nor bureaucrats are held in particularly high esteem, and some doubt the efficacy of the United Nations itself, this building still stands as a beacon of hope that somewhere in the systematic and reasoned arrangement of people, things and their relations we might be able to find a better and more beautiful world. It is a truly modern symbol that sums up the transformation of the modern world from one of warring states to one of networks.

> Where the skyscraper monuments of the postwar period may appear to assimilate corporate authority into the symbolic locus of the church and the state (and the mythic power those embody), in actuality these buildings harbor a new, horizontal network of open circuits … This network reaches outside the city and ultimately across the globe, proliferating in lines of transportation and communication that also constitute the space of the new symbolic.[1]

The United Nations complex is a grouping of simple forms carried out with a limited amount of materials and containing only a part—albeit the most important part—of the organization's activities. Yet it manages to represent the ideals and ideas of the United Nations in a manner that its designers could only dream of. What is even more remarkable is that it does so without recourse to the usual panoply of easy metaphors, statues, and sayings etched into marble. Rather, it accomplishes its symbolic task with abstraction, minimal form, and a few expressive gestures. If it breaks some of the rules for the making of good architecture, it gains a degree of accessibility and a complexity of readings that have let it become the visible symbol for the belief in a world connected and at peace.

The U.N. Building is a shining example of modernist architecture. Like all expressions of modernism, it seeks to give shape to the forces that are continually altering our society and our physical environment.[2] Somehow, despite being produced by a rather confused design process, it has managed to rise out of that style and become a building that is as much about modernism as it is modernist. Using the aesthetics of the machine, construction and surfaces honed down by advanced technology to their most minimal nature, it proposes not so much a machine for making a modern world as a symbol of that machinery. As its principal architect, Wallace K. Harrison, said when he started the design process, it is neither an office building nor an international parliament, but a "workshop for peace."[3] If it turns out that the work that goes on in that forge of international democracy is of a bureaucratic nature, then the U.N. Building stands as the symbol of that kind of activity as truly productive, hopeful and good.

The History

A survey of the history of the U.N. Building's design does not give the reader a sense that anything great could emerge from that tortured and sometimes happenstance process. It progressed in fits and starts and in one headlong rush in the spring and summer of 1947, when architects from around the world crowded into a small office in New York to lay out the basic principles around which the whole complex then developed. Since then, the body that is the United Nations has grown as a result of outside conditions and opportunities. Now it stands poised to engage in its first major expansion project in decades, and thus a realization of where it came from might seem in order.

Before there was the United Nations, there was the League of Nations, and its 1926 competition for a headquarters building haunted the early planners of the United Nations. Swiss-born and Paris-based architect Le Corbusier proposed a grouping of highly articulated elements for all the League's various func-

FULLER-TURNER-WALSH-SLATTERY, INC.

UNITED NATIONS PERMANENT HEADQUARTERS

VIEW NO. *110* DATE *Sep 19-4*

LOCATION NO. *9*

tions, strung together with expressive circulation elements. As in the later U.N. Building, the administrative functions stood as a large, flat plane against the water (in that case Lake Léman), while the main meeting space was a splayed volume connected by ramps and galleries to the larger structure. However, the jury was deeply divided, and Le Corbusier's opponents used the fact that he made the mistake of printing the drawings he submitted, rather than presenting ink originals, to torpedo his design. After a messy and tortured process, a rather staid and pompous design was chosen, by Nénot and Lefèvre, Flegenheimer, Broggi and Vágó.[4]

It is impossible to tell whether the United Nations felt that it needed to make up for its predecessor's mistakes in as many ways as possible, and thus the presence of Le Corbusier as at least a member of the design team seemed necessary, but certainly that hero of modernism was part of the U.N. Building's story from the very beginning. He made sure of his role, agitating along the sidelines and writing an unsolicited report to the committee searching for a new home for the new organization in 1946.[5] His inclusion in the team meant that the U.N. Building would be the most complete realized expression of his ideas about the modern city. Yet the fact that Wallace Harrison, then the most important corporate architect in America, led the team also meant that the final design was a corporate version of that vision. Le Corbusier dreamt of buildings as pure forms in an open landscape, machined to perfection. Harrison believed architecture to be a way of housing the realities of the modern world in the most efficient, logical and stylish manner possible.[6] Out of their discussions, and out of the work of an international team of architects, came the strange hybrid of the United Nations complex. A fragment of a perfect world imagined by one of the world's most visionary architects, it is also a perfected version of the efficient machines for housing bureaucracy that organize the reality of the modern world. What gives this compromise force is the theatrical manner in which the public spaces of the complex stage the

A view from the north. The Secretariat rises out of a plot of land on Manhattan's East River that was originally occupied largely by slaughterhouses.

dream of a perfect world at the base of the slab of modernity sliced off the edge of Manhattan.

The U.N. Building started as a real-estate development. Right after the Second World War, a young developer with a big appetite for everything from cigars to real estate, William Zeckendorf, cast his eye on one of the most underdeveloped sites in Manhattan: the area of slaughterhouses and slums along the East River north of 42nd Street. He understood that the development of midtown Manhattan would eventually spread in this direction, while the riverside location would make it an attractive place in which to live and work. Quietly, he began buying up the existing businesses for low prices. As he did so, he asked the architect Wallace Harrison, who had just returned to practice after a wartime stint working with his former patron Nelson A. Rockefeller at the Bureau for the Coordination of Inter-American Affairs (CIAA), to design a vision of what the area could become. Harrison gave Zeckendorf "X City," a collection of glass slabs that would house 7,500 families and provide 6,000 hotel rooms and office space, above a 5,000-car parking garage. The automobile would provide a plinth on which Harrison imagined various cultural facilities, including an egg-shaped concert hall that could accommodate 6,000 listeners. As rendered by Hugh Ferriss, an architect who produced brooding charcoal images of future skyscrapers that managed to shine with an inner light despite their dark tones,[7] "X City" would have been an immense fortress of glass and steel riding the edge of Manhattan while its inhabitants strolled along ramparts free of cars and suffused with culture. This vision informed and filled out the U.N. Building during its whole design process as much as Le Corbusier's preconceptions.[8]

For Zeckendorf had bitten off more than he could chew. His efforts to finance his grand scheme stalled. In the meantime, the United Nations was busy trying to find a site for its new home. It had appointed a Permanent Headquarters Committee under Dr. Eduardo Zuleta Angel of Colombia to guide the process. After its first meetings in San Francisco, the nascent organization had moved to Lake Success, New York, where it operated from temporary and inadequate quarters. The search at first encompassed the world, narrowed down to the United States, and then to the area around New York City. This narrowing of the site possibilities acknowledged that, though this was to be a world body, in the post-War period the focus of both economic and military power—and of popular culture, which would become more and more important—was New York. The island of skyscrapers was not only increasingly the economic center of the world: its democratic grid sprouting a forest of competing skyscrapers had become a shining symbol of everything a modern society could and should achieve.[9]

At the same time, the messy reality of that city, including its slums, its poverty and the sheer chaos of its daily life—what the architect Rem Koolhaas lauds as the "Culture of Congestion"—scared a newly formed site search committee away. They looked at suburban Connecticut, New Jersey and Pennsylvania, and eager communities offered them sylvan sites with a great deal of space. Yet the committee was not satisfied. The United Nations needed to be close to the big city with all its services, culture, housing and transportation facilities. Robert Moses, the planner and New York strongman who had built an empire of infrastructure by constructing and controlling most of the roads, bridges, tunnels and social housing projects in the city, tried to convince them to re-use the site of the 1939 World's Fair in Queens, across the river from Manhattan.[10] He even had Ferriss draw up a vision of low buildings spread throughout the former swamp and connected by colonnades. The search committee took one sniff of the site and declined the offer.

The Rockefeller family, whose patronage of large-scale development in New York had transformed their oil wealth into Manhattan real estate around Rockefeller Center (designed by a team that included Wallace Harrison), even offered a part of their own estate, Pocantico Hills, just north of the city. A delegation from the Headquarters Committee, including Le Corbusier, flew over the site but could not see it for the trees, and Le Corbusier dismissed it as an inaccessible wilderness. Finally, a solution appeared. Harrison, friend of the Rockefellers and by this point also appointed as a member of the team that would design the building, brokered a three-way deal: the Rockefeller family would donate to the United Nations a sum of $8.5 million to buy the "X City" site, on which they had obtained an exclusive option for this purpose from Zeckendorf. Harrison worked the deal and obtained an exception from the U.S. gift tax for his patrons. On 12 December 1946 the new site of the U.N. Building was announced to the world.[11]

Le Corbusier was outraged. He found the 17 acres the United Nations would have at its disposal much too small and was repelled by the character of the slaughterhouses themselves.[12] Others agreed. Lewis Mumford, the leading architecture critic of the time, suggested that a site of 1,000 acres was needed and proposed a giant slum clearance of Lower Manhattan below Washington Square that would leave the U.N. Building terminating the southern end of Fifth Avenue.[13] When Harrison and the U.N. made it clear that the "X City" site would have to do, Le Corbusier changed his tune and agreed to work on the design. He suggested a list of other modernist architects to collaborate with him on the project, but Harrison, by now completely in charge (he was appointed Director of Planning for the United Nations Permanent Headquarters in January 1947), largely ignored his suggestions in favor of a politically calibrated team of less well known architects from various countries that had joined the United Nations. He set up offices in Rockefeller Center and the team started work, assisted by members of the firm he headed, Harrison & Abramovitz, who were to act as Executive Architects.[14]

Harrison was well prepared for this task. His stint working with Nelson Rockefeller at the CIAA had taught him more about international relations than almost any other architect in the world might know. Before that, he had been one of the architects of Rockefeller Center. That complex of office towers rising out of a labyrinth of stores, theaters and transportation infrastructure had been the place where the skyscraper turned from an isolated place of business into a complete new world. Here technology could let us live, work and be entertained in a completely designed, integrated and conditioned reality where reason and imagination conquered gravity, confusion and rote repetition.[15]

Perhaps as important as his work on Rockefeller Center was Harrison's involvement with the 1939 World's Fair in Queens. Here he had built a new symbol for gathering the cultures of the world: the Trylon and Hemisphere. While the former was an abstraction of the skyscraper, the latter was nothing less than a smoothed version of the whole world. One entered it by a long ramp (perhaps a precursor of the ramped stair in the General Assembly Building) to stand in its vast interior as projections, scrims and models

The international Board of Design (from left): Sven Markelius (Sweden), Le Corbusier (France), Vladimir Bodiansky (Soviet Union), Ssu-ch'eng Liang (China), Wallace Harrison (United States, Director of Planning), Oscar Niemeyer (Brazil), G.A. "Guy" Soilleux (Australia), Nikolai Bassov (Soviet Union), Max Abramovitz (United States, Harrison's partner), Ernest Weissman (Yugoslavia), Ernest Cormier (Canada), Jean Antoniades (Greece), and Matthew Nowicki (Poland).

showed the emergence of a new world of gleaming towers and verdant parks, called "Democracy." (Though the Second World War gave the lie to some of these visions, they were repeated, in somewhat less romantic and more capitalist terms, in the exhibits and the giant globe at the heart of the 1964 World's Fair on the same site.[16])

Harrison's assistant, George Dudley, has left a wonderful account of the resulting team design process that took place during a four-month period at the beginning of 1947.[17] This was unprecedented in the way it sought to produce a unified design out of the collective labors of a group of architects drawn from so wide a field, and such an idealistic way of working has not been tried since. Some architects argued that there should be an open competition for such an important project, but the U.N., probably with the fate of the League of Nations in mind, was more interested in using both the political and the meritocratic possibilities of the organization to come up with a select international team.[18]

Harrison envisioned the U.N. Building as a "workshop for peace" that would provide a rational place for the new organization's major functions: a Secretariat for its daily functions; a General Assembly Building for its twice-yearly plenary meetings; a Conference Building for the work of its major committees and councils; a Delegates' Building where the members could hold office. Left out of the 440,000-square-foot programme (of which 350,000 square feet were for offices), which an in-house committee under the direct supervision of the Secretary-General, Trygve Lie, developed, was housing for the delegates and U.N. workers, as well as a library. The latter was soon envisioned as being built later on the site of a small office building on the southwest corner of the site, owned by the New York City Housing Authority, which could not be immediately torn down.

It became clear early on to all the architects that the function of the Secretariat was to house offices. Le Corbusier immediately latched on to this fact to create what was to be the central element of the complex:

a tall, freestanding office building that he saw as a refinement of the New York skyscraper.[19] He had been arguing since he visited New York in 1935 that the thrusting, stone-clad office towers of Manhattan should be rationalized into slabs or cruciform shapes set in a park-like setting. He had proposed that this was the essence of Manhattan, and had designed versions of it for various sites in the world. He now saw his chance to bring it home where it belonged, to the place where the tall office building had come to fruition.[20] Despite various attempts by other designers to propose smaller groupings of slabs instead of one large structure, Le Corbusier's vision remained at the heart of the design from beginning to end. It was perhaps no coincidence that such slabs also had been promised by Harrison in his "X City" scheme, so that the final Secretariat was the core of Harrison's first vision constructed for an idealistic purpose.

The discussions between the architects concerned the placement and orientation of the various elements on the site. It quickly became evident that the tallest building or buildings should be on the southern edge, where the Manhattan bedrock was closest to the surface.[21] The Chinese participant, Ssu-ch'eng Liang, thought the slab should be oriented perpendicular to the river (i.e., north–south) to minimize solar gain and to respond to traditional placement of buildings.[22] He also saw the site as an enclosed compound rather than an open extension of the city. The Swedish city planner Sven Markelius proposed connecting the site with a curving bridge via Roosevelt Island to Queens in order to provide for future U.N.-related housing and development.[23] The Russian delegate, Nikolai Bassov, argued for a more solid, ground-bound building that would provide a monumental counter-

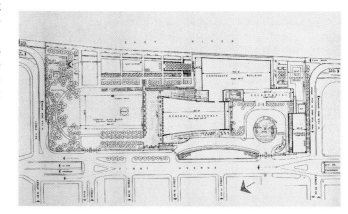

weight to the soaring capitalist skyscrapers around the complex.[24]

In April, Le Corbusier proposed a north–south oriented slab on the southern part of the site, connected to a large square conference building, out of which the General Assembly would emerge to the north as a splayed form gesturing to two east–west oriented slabs for the delegates, which would mark the northern edge of the site. This composition set the tone for the design's further development, but it was the young Brazilian architect Oscar Niemeyer who made the crucial decision, a few weeks later, to express the Assembly Building as a separate entity while pushing the Conference Building to the rear of the site, facing the river. After much jockeying and arguments—Harrison claimed that at one of the meetings Le Corbusier tore all the drawings except his own off the wall and then stomped out (a claim that cannot be verified)[25]—the committee unanimously agreed on a scheme: the Secretariat as a 45-story slab running north–south astride the Conference Building, which in turn was built on piles in the East River over what was to become FDR Drive; the General Assembly Building as a bow tie-shaped object to the north and west, and the two Delegates' Buildings as lower slabs at the northern edge of the complex. Subsequent cost-cutting lopped six floors off the Secretariat, eliminated the Delegates' Buildings (though Harrison built them as private luxury housing in the 1960s), and reduced space in the General Assembly Building, but the $65-million structure was built, with the help of a no-interest loan from the United States Government, as the design team had envisioned it.[26]

The detailed designing became the responsibility of the firm of Harrison & Abramovitz, and they stamped their own aesthetic on the whole complex. Several talented architects contributed to this further development, including Matthew Nowicki, Ernest Weissmann and Kevin Roche, who was later to design the U.N. Plaza Buildings, but most of the interior detailing was done by designers in the office who remain anonymous. Though various other outside architects, as well as artists, contributed interior solutions and objects for various parts of the General Assembly and Conference Buildings, the U.N. Building as it stands today is as much a result of Wallace Harrison's vision as it is of Le Corbusier's. The latter always claimed he was the real designer, and that his architecture had been subsumed by the inferior development of his American friend and collaborator.[27]

The most visible point of disagreement between the two design titans was over the material of the Secretariat. Le Corbusier wanted to cover the two glass façades with a "brise soleil," a stone grid that would provide shade. Harrison and the Americans argued that this would produce dangerous ice build-up and be expensive. They chose Thermapane, a newly developed green glass that filtered the sun. Despite the fact that it would not be needed on the east façade, they decided to use it there as well, creating the distinctive green glass slab that became the U.N.'s signature.[28]

The Building

The result was better than even Le Corbusier expected, though he continued to complain about the finishes for the rest of his life. The planar walls of the Secretariat, 550 feet tall, achieve a high level of abstraction because the architects contained the glass in a neutral grid of aluminum mullions and covered the narrow ends with white marble. These ends serve to heighten the sense that the building is an abstract object on an immense scale, properly contained and framed. The grid of mullions creates a thin, metallic sheen over the façade that breaks up its immense size and catches the light, thus turning the glass mirror into an object with its own materiality and depth. Only the demarcation of the service floors serves to break up the immense and audacious plane that hovers above the East River. Thus the Secretariat becomes both an abstraction of the office grids behind it and an abstract painting itself, posed in front of Manhattan as one approaches from the major airports on Long Island. Here truly is the symbol of a new, rational and abstract world.

The plan shows the relationship among the three original buildings: the bow-tie–shaped General Assembly Building (centre), the Conference Building (by the river, top), and the long, narrow Secretariat (right).

The General Assembly Building is somewhat more problematic. To the west, toward Manhattan, it presents a closed façade of Portland stone (marble was judged too expensive, despite the fact that it was quarried in Vermont, home state of Senator Warren Austin, Chair of the Headquarters Advisory Committee and the United States' major voice in the whole process), from which only escape routes, expressed as ramps that seem to invite entry but do not, emerge (pages 56, 63). The entrance should be, and was originally envisioned as being, on the south façade, where the bow tie flips up to face the large public plaza in front of the Secretariat (page 33). As it is, delegates enter on the west side, and the public on the north side, on what appears to be the complex's back (page 63).[29] There they face a translucent façade, which provides a gentle light on the inside but appears somewhat forbidding from outside. The dome, said to have been added to convince the U.S. Congress, itself housed in a domed symbolic building, to provide the loan for construction, appears incongruous on top of this splayed form.[30] Yet while the architecture appears somewhat illogical, the General Assembly Building has over the years become a slightly enigmatic but all the more powerful symbol of a deliberative body that is not quite a congress and not quite a neutral gathering of conventioneers: for a new kind of organization still trying to define itself, it has proved a tentative, and therefore open-ended, symbol.

It is inside the General Assembly Building and the adjacent Conference Building (which has no exterior of note) that a new world truly opens up. After penetrating the northern façade, visitors emerge into a space whose soaring quality is enhanced by the way in which the concave curve of the balconies recedes while the ramped staircase, balanced on its metal arch, unfurls towards the entrance (page 18). Here the push of theatrical circulation elements, art and interior furnishings plays against the pull of modernist planes that seem to be always receding into a farther distance. The structure and the planes covering that structure are in an active visual dialogue, so that one always feels as if one is backstage in the theater of world relations, with grand set-pieces rising up on all sides.

The Harrison & Abramovitz office detailed every element in these buildings to emphasize their planar quality, to enhance the luxury of precious materials such as marble, bronze and aluminum, and to diffuse any sense of a single, clear focus. Though these are grand, public spaces, they are not monumental in the sense that one is impressed by imposing forms, drawn toward a central focus down a long walkway surrounded by columns, or made to feel insignificant by the clarity of the architectural order all around one. Instead, the building is a collection of fragments. It appears as bits and pieces that define specific moments of circulation, as built-in furniture, fixtures, and areas where one function or the other takes place, without there being a clear hierarchy. This sense of collage increases with the presence of the various artworks that were given by constituent countries, from the Foucault's Pendulum from the Netherlands hanging over the ramped stair to the tapestry from Belgium in the Delegates' Lobby (page 60) and the various murals throughout the lobbies. As a result, the interior of the heart of the United Nations activities combines a sense of elegance, openness and grandeur with a confused complexity that seems—though it is unclear whether this was ever the intention—to reflect the nature of the institution.

The set pieces within this labyrinth of ceremonial spaces, circulation and places to gather or meet one another are the formal meeting rooms. The greatest and most successful of all of these is without a doubt the General Assembly Hall itself (pages 45–51). Though the architects discussed the possible configurations of the seating from the very beginning and at great length, it is actually the space's conical shape that gives it its great and enduring power. The dome, meant to set up echoes of the American palaces of democracy that its initial patrons felt would inspire the rest of the world, recedes high overhead, and it is the slanted wooden slat walls and the recessed gold-

Neither an office building nor an international parliament, but a "workshop for peace."

— WALLACE K. HARRISON,
DIRECTOR OF PLANNING

ABOVE The General Assembly Building under construction.

RIGHT A view of the "back-room boys" working in the 22nd-floor drafting room of the Headquarters Planning Office, 1951.

leaf plane behind the dais that have become the Assembly's iconic emblem. Because of its geometry, the space gathers and weighs on one without making one feel confined or constrained. With the tiers of translators and observers peering through the slats, and the gilt wall looming above the speaker, it seems that the eyes of the world and the promise of a golden future are always upon one.

The three main meeting spaces in the Conference Building are, by contrast, essentially simple boxes in which the architects placed less coherent cages that screen out subsidiary activities and define the focal points within each space. Unfortunately, these rooms make no use of their setting at the edge of the East River, though all have large windows to the view. They also do not have waiting rooms or significant lobbies associated with them to define their importance. Instead, they stand as moments of deliberation in a sea of circulation. Of the three, the Security Council Chamber, though obviously the most important, is also the blandest in its appearance (pages 104–109). Designed by the Norwegian architect Arnstein Arneberg and dominated by a mural painted by his countryman Per Krohg (perhaps the achievement of the first Secretary-General, Trygve Lie, is memorialized in the commissioning of his countrymen to design this important space), its neutral character lets the horseshoe-shaped council table dominate the space.

Finn Juhl, a Danish designer best known for his fluid furniture, gave the Trusteeship Council Chamber—a much larger space—a delicate border of wooden slats that serves to emphasize the breadth of the room (pages 84–91). A large molded white plane floating over the deliberation table creates an implied space within this room where the actual work of the Council took place.

The most effective of these three rooms is the Economic and Social Council Chamber (pages 77–79). Designed by the Swede Sven Markelius, who was part of the original design committee, it shares several devices with the Trusteeship Council Chamber, including the wooden slats on the walls and the sus-

pended ceiling. Here both of these elements are treated with more force, the slats peeling away to show that they are scrims. The ceiling, below which the ducts and electrical chases are left exposed, is painted a dark gray, and Markelius turned the confusion of mechanical equipment into a subtle composition of different hues of that same color. The effect is to make technology a visible and constituent part of the space, while focusing the user's attention on the place of deliberation, carved out as a stage-set for international relations within that framework.

Beyond these ceremonial spaces, the U.N. Building comprises a collection of more or less low-ceilinged, mundane environments. Only the airy expanses of the Delegates' Lobby and the North Delegates' Lounge (pages 60–61, 70–74) capture some sense of the drama reserved for the more formal meeting rooms. However, the Lounge in particular seems as much part of the international style of modern hotel lobbies constructed in the same period around the world as it does an antechamber to the world's parliament. That international style is in fact what the interiors of the U.N.

OPPOSITE, ABOVE The Delegates' Lobby of the General Assembly Building shortly after it was completed (see also pages 60–61).

OPPOSITE, BELOW The public lobby of the General Assembly Building.

ABOVE Surrounded by pre-War buildings (Tudor City) of Manhattan's East Side, the modern Secretariat marks a new era of skyscrapers.

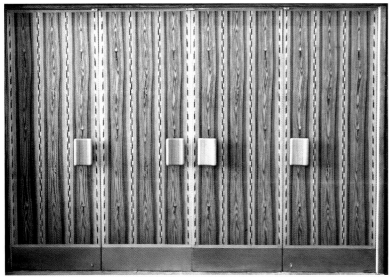

The planning of the U.N. group is a triumph of clarity and ingenuity, a putting together and sorting out of an almost incredible variety of elements and functions. It is also a triumph of technical skill, of structural ability, of mechanical engineering.

– HENRY STERN CHURCHILL, *Architectural Record*, 1953

ABOVE The General Assembly Hall with its original backdrop of discs.

LEFT The doors to the Security Council Chamber, inlaid with ash, with a cross and a sword as decorative motifs. The Chamber was a gift from Norway (see also pages 104–109).

OPPOSITE, ABOVE Looking out over the East River from the Secretariat lobby, 1952.

OPPOSITE, BELOW The terrazzo floor of the Secretariat lobby, 1951.

Building represent at their best: spaces in which new technologies such as steel and concrete construction, electric lighting and air conditioning come together to create open, un-hierarchical spaces where neither the past nor social conventions constrict visitors, while rich materials, often produced or finished by machines, provide a luxurious backdrop to the human actors set free on this open stage on which a new culture was to be played out.[31]

The work of making that new society took and takes places upstairs, in the Secretariat. Internally, its narrow long dimension is broken into parallel lines that were originally all open: long corridors on either side of the elevator and service cores, flanked by the areas where secretaries and support staff worked, and edged by rows of private offices looking out through the glass façades. The simplicity of this design has been lost due to advances in technology, workspace relations and ergonomics—as well as the sheer growth in U.N. staff—but the elongated spaces still prevent the interior from turning into a neutral and hierarchical office landscape.

The addition of the Dag Hammarskjöld Library (pages 142–153) in 1961 completed the complex's overall composition. Though this building is less subtle and energetic in its detailing, it does contain a magnificent reading room, with a curved wooden ceiling that is, though it was designed in the Harrison & Abramovitz office, a tribute to the work of the Finnish architect Alvar Aalto.[32] The building also serves to frame the most dramatic exterior space at the U.N. Building, the circular driveway (page 143). Unfortunately that is only seen by high-level diplomats, but it has entered public consciousness by being portrayed in countless films, television programmes and news bulletins.

The Effect

It is the interpretation of the U.N. Building that has served to make it such a powerful tool in representing the organization and the values for which that stands. There is something about this ensemble that, though it does not always cohere or represent the correct forms of modern architecture, works in an emblematic manner when seen in representations.

The initial reaction to the building upon its completion in 1952 (and even before then, when only the Secretariat was finished) was one of sometimes grudging and even surprised approval. Most critics had not expected this design by committee to work, but most were immediately struck by its effectiveness as image.[33] Typical was the reaction of Lewis Mumford. After criticizing every aspect of the process, from the architect selection to the site to the initial design, he had to admit that it had a certain enchanting quality:

> Here, then, is the Secretariat from the outside: two thin white vertical marble slabs, connected by two vast glass mirrors that are broken only by horizontal white aluminum grilles; a building chaste, startling, fairylike in its cold austerity, a Snow Queen's palace, exhaling by night a green, moonlight splendor.

But, he added, "Paraded as pure engineering and applied geometry, this new skyscraper proves really to be the triumph of irrelevant romanticism."[34]

Philip Johnson, the tastemaker of American architecture for the half century after the Second World War, had said it more simply. The U.N. Building was "by far the best example of modern planning I have seen."[35] The reason for the building's success, most critics agreed, was not its functional clarity or its innovative qualities—though Harrison believed that was what he was trying to achieve—but its formal beauty.[36] As the editors of *Architectural Forum* put it, "The fascination of the Assembly Building lies in its sculptural shape ... It marked an architectural shift from emphasis on function and structural logic to emphasis on form and the logic of art."[37] Mumford had been worried that the architects had "failed to create a fresh symbol" and that the building was all about image:

> Whereas modern architecture began with the precept that form follows function, and that an organic form must respect every human function,

this new building is based on the theory that even if no symbolic purpose is served, function should be sacrificed to form ... Functionally, this building is an old-fashioned engine covered by a streamlined hood embellished with chromium.[38]

Yet it was exactly its ability to present an image that made the building so successful. Perhaps Mumford realized this, for he noted: "If the Secretariat Building will have anything to say as a symbol, it will be, I fear, that the managerial revolution has taken place and that bureaucracy rules the world."[39]

The critic was, of course, right. The building managed to represent bureaucracy—but not as a cold, faceless structure. Instead, the U.N. Building made the work of deliberation, planning, projection, negotiation and implementation seem, if only for a moment, glamorous. By expressing the grid of the Secretariat in isolation, making the General Assembly Building into an enigmatic curve without a clear focus, creating stage-sets for deliberation inside, and making the day-to-day movement around the complex have the glamour of international luxury along with the openness generated by new technology, the architects created a positive image for what could otherwise appear to the public as a rather dull organization. They did so by creating an ensemble that is both neutral and emblematic of a new, systems-oriented kind of governance, one that promised to rationalize and supersede Manhattan and its logic from the foundation that city had established. As the architect Rem Koolhaas put it years later,

> As Le Corbusier tried to drain Manhattan of congestion, so Harrison now drains Le Corbusier's Ville Radieuse [his scheme for a city of skyscrapers set in a green park] of ideology. In his sensitive and professional hands, the abstract abrasiveness mellows to the point where the entire complex becomes merely one of Manhattan's enclaves, a block like the others, one isolated island of Manhattan's ideology.[40]

OPPOSITE, ABOVE AND BELOW The North Delegates' Lounge in its original incarnation (see also pages 70–74).

ABOVE The United Nations programme board showing the time and location of meetings and conferences.

RIGHT A U.N. employee at the "starter control panel" of a bank of elevators in the Secretariat, 1951. The panels moderated the complex flow of vertical traffic according to the movement of people and the time of day.

OPPOSITE A glimpse inside an interpreters' booth as they were originally used in the 1950s.

The U.N. Building, in other words, is architecture shorn of ideology, but shorn also of the thrusting and competitive individualism of New York's skyscrapers.

That sense of excitement certainly was picked up by those looking for settings in which they could tell stories about the future, our faith in it, and the dangers that could turn such dreams into nightmares. The most famous images of the U.N. Building undoubtedly come from Alfred Hitchcock's great masterpiece, the 1959 film *North by Northwest*. The building (recreated on a set, as the producers could not obtain permission to film in it) figures at a crucial point in the plot, when Cary Grant witnesses a murder and realizes that his life is in danger. The excitement inherent in this enclave of the international world is both exhilarating, as the building towers over the actors, and dangerous, as it becomes clear that all is not well in those international relations. The modernist image hides a darker reality. Hitchcock exploited the building's angular geometries to the fullest, making us realize that here was a world out of the ordinary, pointing the way, often quite literally, to north by northwest, where justice would prevail.

In 1953, the U.N. Building figured in the film *The Glass Wall* as the place where a European refugee could argue his case for being in the United States. The building gave the film its title. It is the place that stands for international justice, but also for a refined version of the American freedom for which the refugee yearns. In countless other films, documentaries and newsreels, the U.N. Building has a similar function, if only as a backdrop to demonstrations: it is the place that symbolizes freedom, justice, and solutions to specific local problems through a grid-like, mirror-like deliberative process. Meanwhile, the 1977 Disney cartoon *The Rescuers* shows the building as the headquarters of the International Rescue Aid Society, an organization of mice for whom the modern grandeur of the U.N. is all the more exhilarating because of their perspective.

Because of the U.N. Building's power as a symbol, it is also often under threat in the media. Superman goes to the U.N. in 1987 (in *Superman IV*) to promise the assembled countries that he will rid the world of nuclear weapons, only to be forced to protect the world from dastardly threats. Wonder Woman has to save the U.N. twice (*Wonder Woman #217*, 1975, and *Wonder Woman #262*, 1979) from threats to blow it up, as does George Clooney in the 1997 film *The Peacemaker*. It is only Inspector Dreyfus who manages to

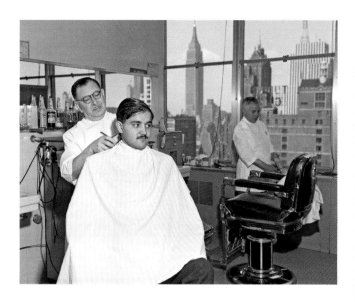

blow the building up, in the 1976 film *The Pink Panther Strikes Again*.

Yet the U.N. Building has survived, and in *The Interpreter* of 2005 it can still stand as a symbol of justice achieved through deliberation, agreement, due process and even forgiveness. In the first film for which the U.N. gave permission to use the building as location, the hopes for a better future and the dangers lurking within the very process that will get us to that place have found an eerie, confusing and ultimately safe home. The film makes full use of both the theatrical glamour and the confusion inherent in the building's design, and the way it forces resolution out of confrontation. Ending in the "safe room" behind the General Assembly Hall, it lets the structure serve as a cocoon around political violence—though it is the decisions made by the actors, not the building itself, that create peace and reconciliation. The building remains immutable, usable in different ways, but intact as a set piece and a symbol that frames the actor's search for truth and justice.

To many artists and photographers, that faith in the U.N. Building's efficacy has a slightly nostalgic tinge. It has become the subject of many photographs and paintings that show New York at twilight or dawn, dramatizing the sense of a new world rising or left behind as an empty symbol as the world fades into night. In the last few years, photographers have delved into the building's interiors, finding in its so carefully studied, but now worn and slightly quaint, compositions images that make us remember nothing so much as the promise the past felt the future once held.

The U.N. Building has also, to a certain extent, lost its promise as a building. It does seem somewhat dated. Expansions, such as the U.N. Plaza Buildings to the west, have had the result of integrating it into the fabric of the city, with the ironic effect of making it seem somewhat less special. At the same time, new security measures have made the experience of the U.N. Building something one attains only after being confronted with the realities of a world that is indeed still not at peace. Much is off limits to the public and

ABOVE The original barber shop on the 20th floor of the Secretariat, shown here with the Barbagallo brothers—the barbers—and Ansar Khan, a staff member from Pakistan, having his hair cut.

BELOW An army of cleaners begin their work on the 2 million square feet of flooring. The three-stemmed floor lamps in the background are a distinctive design feature of the Conference Building (see also pages 71 and 141).

much of it also has been altered to the point where it has lost its original verve.

The U.N. Building somehow manages to rise above all this with its cold, bureaucratic majesty, its theatrical confusion of forms, and its abstract symbolism. It might not embody either the architecture or the polity of our dreams, but it does house the one organization that seeks to build a better future within a building that keeps staging that future in its architecture of idealistic organization.

Rotterdam, 2005

ABOVE The information booth in the public lobby of the General Assembly Building (see also page 37).

BELOW Light cascades into the lobby of the Secretariat, which faces Manhattan's East River, in 1952. There is no longer an information booth in the Secretariat.

Notes

1 Reinhold Martin, *The Organization Complex: Architecture, Media and Corporate Space* (Cambridge, Mass.: The MIT Press, 2003), p. 7.

2 I use here Marshall Berman's definition in his *All That Is Solid Melts Into Air: The Experience of Modernity* (New York: Simon & Schuster, 1982), pp 15ff.

3 Quoted in *The New York Herald*, 22 May 1947, p. 1.

4 Cf. Stanislaus von Moos, *Le Corbusier, Elements of a Synthesis* (Cambridge, Mass.: The MIT Press, 1979), pp 239ff.

5 Robert A. M. Stern, Thomas Mellins, David Fishman, *New York 1960: Architecture and Urbanism Between the Second World War and the Bicentennial* (New York: The Monacelli Press, 1995), p. 609.

6 For Le Corbusier's attitude towards New York, see Rem Koolhaas, *Delirious New York: A Retroactive Manifesto for New York* (New York: The Monacelli Press, 1994 [1977]), pp 255ff. For a keen and thorough analysis of Wallace Harrison's architecture, see Victoria Newhouse, *Wallace K. Harrison, Architect* (New York: Rizzoli International Publications, 1989).

7 Ferriss later also played an important role in presenting the design to the public. It could be said that his visions, which exist as a kind of force behind much of late-20th-century New York architecture, are as much part of the genesis of the U.N. Building's designs as the ideas of the designers themselves. For Ferriss's own vision of what an ideal city might look like, see his *The Metropolis of Tomorrow* (Dover Books, 1986 [1929]).

8 *Wallace K. Harrison*, pp 104–6; *New York 1960*, pp 606–8.

9 *New York 1960*, pp 604–6. See also the Archives of the United Nations, Scrapbooks.

10 *New York 1960*, pp 601–4. For the role Robert Moses played in New York architecture and urbanism, see Robert Caro's seminal *The Power Broker: Robert Moses and the Fall of New York* (New York: Alfred A. Knopf, 1974). George Dudley (see below) often refers to Harrison having to meet Moses to keep the design process on track.

11 *New York 1960*, p. 607.

12 Ibid.; *Wallace K. Harrison*, pp 108–12.

13 Lewis Mumford, "U.N. Model and Model U.N.," in *From the Ground Up: Observations on Contemporary Architecture, Housing, Highway Building and Civic Design* (New York, Harvest Books, 1956), pp 2–26, p. 22.

14 *Wallace K. Harrison*, pp 112–13.

15 Cf. *Delirious New York*, pp 161–234; *Wallace K. Harrison*, pp 34–55; Daniel Okrent, *Great Fortune: The Epic of Rockefeller Center* (New York: Viking Press, 2003).

16 *Wallace K. Harrison*, pp 80–93; *New York 1960*, pp 1027–57. See also Erik Mattie, *World's Fairs* (New York: Princeton Architectural Press, 1998). For a wonderful view on its meaning, see David Gelernter, *1939: The Lost World of the Fair* (New York: Free Press, 1995).

17 George A. Dudley, *A Workshop of Peace: Designing the United Nations Headquarters* (New York: The Architectural History Foundation, 1994).

18 *New York 1960*, p. 604.

19 Ibid., p. 17.

20 Le Corbusier, *Quand les Cathédrales étaient blanches* (Paris, 1937), translated as *When the Cathedrals Where White* (New York: McGraw Hill, 1964); *Le Corbusier*, pp. 207–10.

21 Undated note, Archives of the United Nations, New York Headquarters Building Collection.

22 *Workshop*, pp 170ff.

23 Ibid., pp 214ff.

24 Ibid., p. 232.

25 *Wallace K. Harrison*, p. 120.

26 Dudley summarizes the development of these schemes very neatly with a diagram on pp 226–27 of *Workshop*.

27 Le Corbusier, *Oeuvre Complète 1946–1952* (Basel: Birkhäuser, 1955), p. 39; *Le Corbusier*, p. 250; *Wallace K. Harrison*, p. 127.

28 *New York 1960*, p. 618, *Wallace K. Harrison*, p. 127.

29 Though Dudley traces the intricate discussions about the placement of the various elements, it is not clear from any of the discussions why the entrance was moved to the north. The designers were extremely concerned about separating the flow of visitors, delegates and press, and perhaps this was the default solution.

30 *New York 1960*, p. 613.

31 Paul Rudolph, then a young architect, said of the interior: "Of course the building is not really a product of the International Style but rather a background for a grade 'B' movie about 'one world' with Rita Hayworth dancing up the main ramp." *New York 1960*, p. 623.

32 It should be noted that Aalto was excluded from the original design process because Finland was not a member of the United Nations. Famous German architects such as Ludwig Mies van der Rohe and Walter Gropius were excluded for the same reason.

33 *The New York Times* editors on 17 September 1947 called it "a city made largely of glass."

34 Lewis Mumford, "Magic with Mirrors," in: *From the Ground Up*, op. cit., pp 36–44.

35 Quoted in *The New York Times*, 13 August 1947.

36 Harrison defended his design in Edgar Snow, "World Capital on Turtle Bay," in *The Saturday Evening Post*, June 1947, pp 27, 29, 108–13: "The real symbol of a building comes out of what is done in it, not what it done to the outside of it … I've been through all the set-ups—classical, Greek, Roman, Gothic, neoclassical and so on. I've tried 'em all. Out of it I've learned just this: if you build for the needs of the human beings who use the place, you get a symbol that expresses the period" (p. 111).

37 "United Nations Building," in *Architectural Forum*, May 1950, p. 97.

38 Lewis Mumford, "Magic with Mirrors," in *From the Ground Up*, op. cit., p. 37.

39 Lewis Mumford, "Buildings As Symbols," in *From the Ground Up*, op. cit., p. 30.

40 *Delirious New York*, op. cit., p. 281.

OPPOSITE Rarely seen views of the suite and private apartment of the second Secretary-General, Dag Hammarskjöld, in the Secretariat, which includes living and dining rooms and office (see also pages 122–127). CENTER, the living room in 1953; ABOVE AND BELOW, the office in 1961.

Photographer's Note

BEN MURPHY

My decision to photograph the U.N. Building emerged from a conversation with a writer friend living in New York. I am always looking for places that contain a strong sense of history and convey an atmosphere of the past, to investigate the idea of impermanence and the places we build to make a secure environment for living and working. I am intrigued by the notion that no matter what monuments we construct, nothing can keep us from rebuilding our surroundings. It was in this light that the U.N. Building was suggested, and after months of negotiations, I was privileged to have been given permission to document this extraordinary place.

The U.N. Building appeals to me aesthetically and philosophically. Abutting the East River in midtown Manhattan, this iconic modernist masterpiece symbolizes a futuristic post-war optimism that envisioned peaceful cooperation throughout the world. It is impossible for visitors not to be moved by the imposing architecture and the beauty of its interiors, despite an obvious need for certain modernization and restoration. It is a paradox that an organization at the centre of world politics is operating out of a building designed for a different age. Despite the power of its visual symbolism and architectural significance, there is a need for change, but this makes it all the more fascinating.

The aspects of the building that made it attractive to me as a photographer, however, may be lost in the renovation and modernization work that is expected to begin in 2007. What made my documentation more poignant for me was that much of what I photographed will be removed, replaced or altered forever. No matter how sensitively the intended refurbishment programme is carried out, the building's character will be changed by the installation of new technologies and updated security and safety measures; practicality will take precedence over aesthetics. All of the work is necessary to bring the building up to date, but my personal preference would be for nature to take its course, to witness the building age gracefully without interference. I know that this is not a feasible option, though, and to survive there must be evolution.

Over a period of fifteen months I photographed everything I found appealing, from seemingly incidental details that are easily overlooked—such as hearing devices and old recording equipment—to design features in the wood-paneled walls, textures and patterns, the endless sweeping corridors with their highly polished floors, and the vast, otherworldly theatrical spaces of the main conference rooms. I also focused on the more rarely seen places and their quieter atmospheres, each room and object contributing to the U.N.'s unique character.

Even though the rooms are occupied during the day and the corridors are as full of traffic as the New York streets outside, I chose to photograph the interiors empty, because by concentrating on what is left behind in people's absence one gains a better impression of what these spaces represent. In the General Assembly Hall, for example, a green marble podium stands at the front of the stage, with an enormous wall of gold leaf acting as a backdrop, set with the immediately recognizable symbol of the U.N. On the floor, carefully color-coordinated seats attentively face the stage. Every aspect of this, the U.N.'s heart, is dressed to give the impression of greatness.

There is an undeniably religious air within the hall, a temple to politics with diplomacy its central text. Scattered around the desks in this and other rooms are the small pale-blue booklets containing the U.N.'s charter. The General Assembly Hall is a theater of ceremony. Politicians, like actors and playwrights, need their stages. In the still of the waiting rooms behind the General Assembly Hall, I try to imagine all the world leaders who have sat in these chairs gazing up at the elongated map of the world before going onto the podium to speak.

Architecture and the space that surrounds us profoundly affects and controls our emotions. The atmosphere established here by the building's construction and those who have occupied it influenced my decisions about what to photograph, just as this aura must have affected, consciously or subconsciously, the thoughts of the thousands of delegates who have participated in the hall's proceedings.

Walking into the U.N. Building is like being drawn into a childhood storybook depicting a science-fiction fantasy world where anything is possible. The difference here, of course, is that this is a real place, where decisions are made that affect entire nations.

It is important that a visual record of the building is made before major alterations begin, and although I approached this project from an individual perspective and my photographs represent a personal response, my hope is that by documenting what I found interesting I have helped to preserve a memory for the future.

London, 2005

The U.N. Building

PHOTOGRAPHS BY BEN MURPHY

The pictures on the following pages were taken
between October 2003 and January 2005. Because
of the size and complexity of the U.N. Building,
a number of spaces have been renovated,
remodeled or refurbished, though many retain
their original features and pieces. In a few
instances, some rooms are no longer as they are
depicted in this book. An extensive restoration
of the buildings is expected to begin in 2007.

Situated on Manhattan's East Side, with the Queensboro Bridge in the distance to the north, the United Nations Headquarters comprises six buildings on an 18-acre, 6-block tract between 42nd and 48th Streets and First Avenue and the East River. The original complex, which included the domed General Assembly Building (center left), the Secretariat tower, and the waterfront Conference Building connecting the two, was completed in the early 1950s.

Wallace K. Harrison was the architect responsible for bringing an international design team and the buildings together into a unified whole. The Dag Hammarskjöld Library (bottom) was the first major addition to the original design. Later, the North Lawn was created underground to contain the reproduction (printing) plant; along the river, on the southeast corner of the complex, the South Annex (bottom right) was constructed to house the staff cafeteria.

GENERAL ASSEMBLY BUILDING

The form of the 39-story Secretariat—designed to be 45 stories high before budget constraints forced the loss of six levels—was largely influenced by the vision of modern master Le Corbusier, reconciled through his former employee Oscar Niemeyer, also a member of the design team. Complete in 1950, it was one of the world's first largely glass skyscrapers, with 5,200 openable windows and 20 acres of office space, made flexible through movable metal partitions.

A bronze sculpture by British artist Barbara Hepworth, *Single Form* (1964), is the centerpiece of the circular forecourt that connects the buildings. It and the Library (at right) commemorate the U.N.'s second Secretary-General, Dag Hammarskjöld, a friend and admirer of the sculptor. Hepworth intended her piece, which took twenty months to complete and stands 21 feet tall, to embody Hammarskjöld's "human aesthetic ideology" and "to perfect a symbol that would reflect the nobility of his life."

Visitors to the General Assembly Building, completed in 1952, are greeted by the scalloped form of the information kiosk in the lobby.

For the people who have lived through Dunkerque, Warsaw, Stalingrad and Hiroshima, may we build so simply, honestly and cleanly that it will inspire the United Nations, who are today building a new world, to build this world on the same pattern.

— WALLACE K. HARRISON, 1947

PREVIOUS PAGES, LEFT
An interior detail of the public lobby shows the glass façade, between the piers of which were set seven nickel and bronze doors with bas-reliefs donated by Canada in 1953. Above the doors, specially designed translucent glass panels were intended to introduce cathedral-like natural light into the space.

PREVIOUS PAGES, RIGHT
The sweeping interior ramps and cantilevered balconies animate the lofty public lobby of the General Assembly Building (see also page 18).

ABOVE

On one of the public lobby's balconies outside the General Assembly Hall, a leather sofa and chairs, gifts from Thailand in 1954, provide points of repose. True to the international character of the organization, a good deal of the furnishings, fittings and artworks have been donated from around the world.

OPPOSITE

On the north balcony, the General Assembly Hall's imposing doors, inset with circular handles and framed by marble panels, offer the first hint of the grandeur beyond. This entrance, reserved for selected high officials, kings and queens, is rarely used; the last occasion was in 1979 by Pope John Paul II. After ascending the lobby's sweeping stairs, the speaker passes through these doors into what is informally called the "bull run"—a fairly long, dark, steep corridor—to emerge in the center of the General Assembly Hall, directly across from the rostrum, as captured by the photograph on page 49.

Everything will be alright when people stop thinking of the United Nations as a weird Picasso abstraction and see it as a drawing they made themselves.

– DAG HAMMARSKJÖLD

The rostrum of the majestic General Assembly has hosted virtually every head of state and diplomatic luminary since it was first convened on 14 October 1952. The sloping backdrop, to which was originally applied an ornamental grid of disc-shaped lights (page 20), was later covered in shimmering gold leaf because television crews and photographers were unable to capture high-quality images of the speakers. Fronted by distinctive dark green marble, the three seats below the U.N. emblem are occupied by the President of the General Assembly, the Secretary-General, and the Under-Secretary-General for General Assembly and Conference Management.

The design of the United Nations emblem was approved by the General Assembly on 7 December 1946. It consists of a map of the world (on a polar azimuthal equidistant projection) surrounded by two olive branches—symbols of peace—and displayed over five concentric circles.

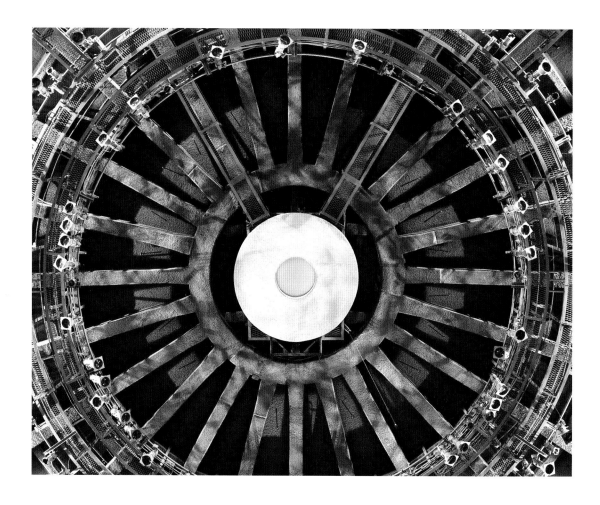

PREVIOUS PAGES
The General Assembly Hall represents the true collaboration of the original design team's eleven architects, after extensive research into parliaments around the world in order to derive an ideal form for the "parliament of nations." Wallace K. Harrison, leading the team, reflected on the building in later life: "I and the others expressed the Assembly with the slope of the roof and walls. Does it go with the office building [Secretariat]? Perhaps not, but how do you do it better?" Lending particular warmth to a hall that seats almost 2,000 delegates from 191 Member States are the elegant slanting walls made of mahogany battens covered with copper alloy. Apart from their aesthetic effect, the slats concealed a variety of technologies that were advanced for the time.

The hall accommodates delegations, each with six seats for three full delegates (beige chairs) and three for alternates (blue chairs). Most of the seats are in the main hall; further seats are in the stepped platforms rising from the rear and in the galleries and balconies of the upper floors, where certain seats and rows are reserved for representatives of the news media and for the public. On the tables in front of each delegation are green, red and yellow buttons, which indicate votes for, against, or abstentions from resolutions. Countries are equally represented in the U.N. main deliberative body: one member, one vote. Interpreters translating into one of the United Nations six official languages (Arabic, Chinese, English, French, Russian, and Spanish), official verbatim reporters, television cameramen and other technicians occupy glass-fronted rooms that overlook the space.

ABOVE
The hall is crowned by a dome, a typical feature of American governmental buildings, which, it has been suggested, may have been added to the design to gain U.S. congressional approval for a loan when funds for the project ran low.

FOLLOWING PAGES
The abstract murals on either side are an anonymous gift. Originally designed by Fernand Léger, they were painted by Bruce Gregory, one of his pupils.

Here is a building that represents an intuitive series of treatments rather than the development of a closely reasoned scheme; a series of episodes rather than a close-knit event ... What is depended on to hold it all together is taste, judgment, personality.

– Architectural Forum, 1952

The GA 200 reception room prior to its renovation in 2004 (for its present appearance, see pages 158–159). On the wall is a clock designed and built by Derby, of Neufchâtel, Switzerland, in the form of a world map showing official time zones and capitals of the Member States, a gift from the watch-makers of that country in 1969.

Located behind the podium of the General Assembly Hall, the GA 200 is the only enclosed space in the General Assembly Building (hence its mysterious name: "GA" for General Assembly, "2" for the second floor, "00" because there are no other rooms on that floor). It derives its great importance from being the space where heads of state convene prior to delivering their speeches to the General Assembly. Private talks and meetings with the Secretary-General are also conducted here. The GA 200 also includes a lounge, press area and offices.

Use it, respect it, defend it. It can be no wiser, no more competent and no more efficient than those Member States that now comprise and guide it.

– KOFI A. ANNAN, 1996

The GA 200 meeting room prior to the 2004 renovation. On the wall hangs an oil painting by the Icelandic artist Johannes Kjarval, a gift of Iceland in 1985. It depicts the landscape of Thingvellir, site of Iceland's National Parliament founded in 930 CE.

On 20 October 1947 the General Assembly agreed that the flag of the United Nations would feature the official emblem on a light-blue background. In so far as is known, the colour has no special significance.

The sculptural form of the General Assembly Building's curved roof and walls was an unexpected departure from the dominant rectilinear aesthetic of the International Style. The curve is indeed the building's distinctive feature outside and in (the Assembly Hall is completely non-rectilinear, including the juncture of wall and floor). The walls are clad in Portland stone and framed by the same marble that covers the end walls of the Secretariat. The dome was a later addition to the design; the two-level ramp is an emergency exit.

In contrast to the curving east and west walls and roof of the
General Assembly Building, its south side is a huge plate-glass
window, 53½ feet high, set in a deeply recessed marble frame through
which the delegates' entrance and lobby are visible (see also pages
18 and 60–61). The all-glass façade, turned toward the Secretariat
and Library, shares their architectural language of bold geometry
and transparency.

A satellite dish in the grounds is a reminder of the global communication system that links the United Nations Headquarters in New York with its offices and operations overseas.

ABOVE
One of two twin information desks in the spacious Delegates' Entrance, located on the west side of the General Assembly Building (on First Avenue).

OPPOSITE
The majestic Delegates' Lobby in the General Assembly Building (see also page 18). The intense natural light and high ceiling called for artworks of imposing dimensions: on the north wall (at right) is the tapestry *Triumph of Peace*, a gift from Belgium in 1954. Designed by Peter Colfs, it was executed by fourteen craftsmen who used 94,000 miles of yarn. It is one of the largest tapestries in the world, measuring 43½ by 28½ feet. On the west wall (at left) is *Peace*, one of two murals by Candido Portinari; *War* hangs on the opposite wall. Donated by Brazil in 1957, the oil-on-cedar murals measure 34 by 46 feet. Stairs and escalators lead up from the Delegates' Entrance. Beyond them is the curtained Indonesian Lounge, with the Express Bar above it.

According to myth, Wallace Harrison was the "bad" corporate architect—if not simply a hack—who stole Le Corbusier's design for the United Nations building (1947–50) and made it mediocre reality. This myth was sufficiently established to prevent anyone from taking a serious look at the building itself. But a closer inspection of the dry theoretical pretension of Le Corbusier's proposition and the polymorphously perverse professionalism with which Harrison realized it suggested, if not a reversal of the myth, a rewriting: the U.N. was a building that an American could never have thought and a European could never have built. It was a collaboration, not only between two architects, but between cultures; a cross-fertilization between Europe and America produced a hybrid that could not have existed without their mating, however unenthusiastic.

— REM KOOLHAAS

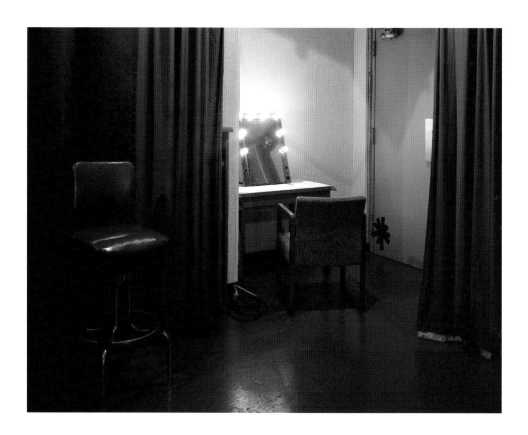

TV studio H with its make-up room (ABOVE), in the General Assembly Building, is the main studio used for taping messages and for the production of live broadcast feeds. Different sets can be used: the one shown here (OPPOSITE) is well known and has contributed to turn the U.N. flag and the characteristic blue curtain into familiar symbols. United Nations Television produces and distributes coverage of events at the Headquarters and creates programmes for international distribution, including "United Nations in Action" and "World Chronicle" (www.un.org/webcast), as well as video documentaries, public service announcements and short features (www.un.org/av/tv). Some 90 television stations in 40 countries, with an estimated audience reach of a billion, benefit from United Nations programming.

One of the five radio studios used for news, current affairs, in-depth feature and documentary programming—in both official and non-official languages—on United Nations issues, conferences and thematic events. Since 2000, a daily live 15-minute programme has been produced in the U.N.'s official languages and distributed to 174 radio stations in 75 countries, with an estimated audience of over 130 million. The website is www.un.org/radio.

FOLLOWING PAGES
A glimpse into the International Broadcasting Centre (IBC), the main control room for incoming and outgoing feeds for the U.N.'s radio and television broadcasts.

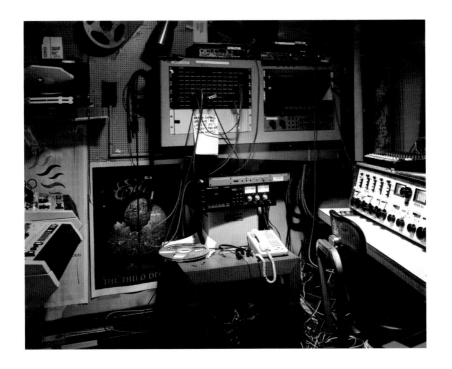

CONFERENCE BUILDING

The Conference Building, completed in 1952, stretches 400 feet along the East River and forms a connection between the Secretariat and the General Assembly Building. Occupying a well illuminated double-height corner space in the building, the North Delegates' Lounge capitalizes on the natural light and views across the River and north into Manhattan.

Many of the modern pieces of furniture and light fittings, such as the copies of Mies van der Rohe's Barcelona Chair, the Knoll club chairs and the three-stemmed floor lamps, are original to the building. The latter, particularly numerous in the corridors outside the conference rooms, are a distinctive landmark of the Conference Building (see page 141).

Adorning the south wall of the North Delegates' Lounge is a 30-foot-long tapestry of the Great Wall, given to the United Nations by China in 1974. Made with more than 50,000 yards of wool and half a million knots, it weighs more than 600 pounds. It is one of over three hundred gifts to the U.N. offered mainly by Member States but also by foundations, associations, private and sometimes anonymous individuals. Donations are displayed throughout the complex, but many are in storage because of lack of space.

The sculptural form of the wooden bar is the centerpiece of the
mezzanine in the North Delegates' Lounge.

A glimpse of the United Nations Correspondents Association (UNCA) Club, established in 1948. In the room, in the club's own words, "we have interrogated and entertained dissidents, statesmen and stateswomen, ambassadors, international civil servants and fellow journalists." The portraits around the top are of UNCA presidents, who have always held the privilege of asking the first question at U.N. press conferences. The smaller pictures below them, dating from the 1950s and 1960s, show the U.N. press corps at work with international figures, such as Nikita Khrushchev. The room was remodeled in 1998 with the help of the American furniture company Ethan Allen.

In front of the press corps (at left) stands a solitary microphone, which is often at the center of international issues. The Security Council "stake-out" is a gathering place directly outside the entrance to the Chamber for the press to interview delegates to the Council. In recent years, the microphone has been placed in front of a backdrop featuring the flags of the U.N. and Council members. Over 3,600 journalists are permanently accredited to the United Nations and over 10,000 are present during major meetings.

Economic and Social Council Chamber

The Economic and Social Council—referred to internally as 'ECOSOC'—was established as the primary organ to coordinate programmes in social development, promoting human rights, spreading the benefits of science and technology, ensuring the status of women, and crime prevention, among other activities. The Council has fifty-four members.

Like the other two major assembly rooms in the Conference Building—the Trusteeship Council Chamber and the Security Council Chamber—the Economic and Social Council Chamber includes seats for the public and members of the press.

The Economic and Social Council Chamber was designed by the architect Sven Markelius, who was also a member of the U.N. complex original design team. The Swedish government donated the furnishings and the pine used in the slatted cladding, as well as the magnificent tapestry hand-woven in the southern part of the country. The ceiling, which in the delegates' area (LEFT) is suspended and highly stylized, is purposely dark and unfinished in the public gallery area to symbolize that the work of this Council is ongoing. Some changes were made to the original design in 1974, when the number of Council members doubled from twenty-seven to fifty-four. Sweden renovated the Chamber in 1995 as a gift to the U.N. for its fiftieth anniversary.

Behind the central scenes of the Economic and Social Council Chamber are the interpreters' booths and sound-recording studios.

Next to the Security Council Chamber is the "Quiet Room," with its distinctive diagonal panelling, furniture and carpeting, which was a gift to the United Nations from the Federal Republic of Germany in 1978. The interior designers Günter Fruhtrunk and Paolo Nestler won a national competition to create the space. Upon its inauguration, the German ambassador said, "As I myself look at these walls—without being either an architect or an artist—I recall a sentence from the writings of Le Corbusier, where he says: 'We'll get the painters in to blow up the walls that stand in our way.' This, to my mind, is exactly what has been achieved here." Accessible to delegates only, the Quiet Room is part of the Security Council's "quarters," which include the President's Office, the Consultation Room (page 110) and the smaller, more private Caucus Room.

Trusteeship Council Chamber

Continuing the Scandinavian interior scheme of the Economic and Social Council Chamber (pages 77–79), the clean lines and pleasing colours of the Trusteeship Council Chamber were provided by Denmark and designed by the architect Finn Juhl. The chamber is clad in strips of ash to provide acoustical support and has a beauty and warmth all its own. The network of wooden battens suspended below the mechanical ceiling had a great influence on the design of shop interiors in the 1950s. The Trusteeship Council was established to promote the political, economic and social development of nations that were largely under colonial rule. The aim of returning self-government to these "Trust Territories" has now been largely fulfilled.

PREVIOUS PAGES and OPPOSITE
Two paintings adorn the Trusteeship Council Chamber: on the left
wall is *Codice del Fuego* (Fire Codex), a three-panel painting
presented by Ecuador, inspired by pre-Columbian mythology and
colors; on the right wall is *Gandzelo* (Sacred Tree), presented by
Mozambique in 1997 to commemorate the role of the United Nations
in restoring peace to the war-ravaged country.

To those outside who question us we can reply: we are united, we are a team; the World Team of the United Nations laying down the plans of a world architecture, *world*, not *international*, for therein we shall respect the human, natural and cosmic laws.... There are no names attached to this work. As in any human enterprise, there is simply discipline, which alone is capable of bringing order.

— LE CORBUSIER

PAGES 92–97
The United Nations employs approximately 140 interpreters. They usually interpret for thirty minutes at a time and take turns, with three normally assigned to each language booth. Early in 1946, the General Assembly established Chinese, English, French, Russian, and Spanish as the official languages of the organization, with English and French as working languages. Arabic has been an official language since 1973. Simultaneous interpretation into the six official languages is provided in all U.N. meetings. The equipment used by delegates and their interpreters is standard in the many conference rooms throughout the complex.

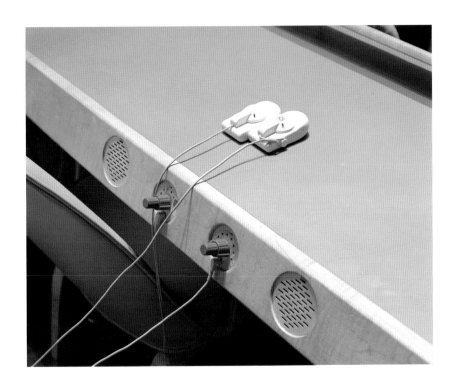

Conference Room 8 is also called the "United Kingdom Room," as that country donated all the furnishings in 1951. Animals and flowers are carved on the oak-panelled walls, tables and chairs are of English oak, and a green carpet covers the floor. Seats for thirty-three surround the table; another sixty-four can fill the space.

Some of the building's most endearing features are in the
details, such as the vintage clocks or exit signs that might
be overlooked during discussion, and yet they very quietly
evoke the era in which the building was designed and
built. The original IBM office clocks with radio vacuum
tube (top) were originally synchronized, at five minutes
to the hour, by a central signal.

The conference officer table, at left, in Conference Room 8. The service desk's function is to distribute documents and messages in each conference room.

Security Council Chamber

Witness to some of the most momentous discussions and decisions since the Second World War, the Security Council Chamber is perhaps the most recognizable space of the entire Headquarters. The Council is composed of fifteen member countries: five permanent—China, France, the Russian Federation, the United Kingdom and the United States—and ten who are elected by the General Assembly for two-year terms. Decisions on important matters require nine votes including a unanimity of votes from the five permanent members, any one of which can therefore veto a resolution. The Council may invite speakers to debate an issue; equally, any State (whether or not a member of the U.N.), the General Assembly, or the Secretary-General may bring matters to the Council's attention.

The chamber was designed by Arnstein Arneberg, the architect of Oslo's City Hall, and was a gift of Norway. Its backdrop is a mural by Arnenberg's compatriot Per Krohg. "I have tried not to use the ordinary hackneyed symbols," he said. "Freedom is a man taking a horse's bit and letting him run free in the green meadows. Brotherhood is shown by the union of nations and races in the central panel at the top. The whole is lit by the sun's rays. A small horizontal panel at the top, which I call the New Renaissance, contains all the arts happily united, the men who interpret events and develop them, those who write history."

This inlaid door of Norwegian ash leads to the office of the President of the Security Council (see also page 20). Each member of the Council serves as President for one month in turn (in English alphabetical order). In contrast, the President of the General Assembly, elected at the beginning of each session, changes on an annual basis. He or she serves as an individual, not as a representative of his or her country.

The blue-and-gold silk tapestry on the walls and in the draperies
depicts the anchor of faith, the growing wheat of hope, and the heart
of charity. The red chairs are for Member States' delegates who are
not at that moment members of the Security Council.

Overlooking the delegates' level in the Security Council Chamber are
164 green seats for public viewers and 118 green seats for members
of the press (the chairs with desk arms).

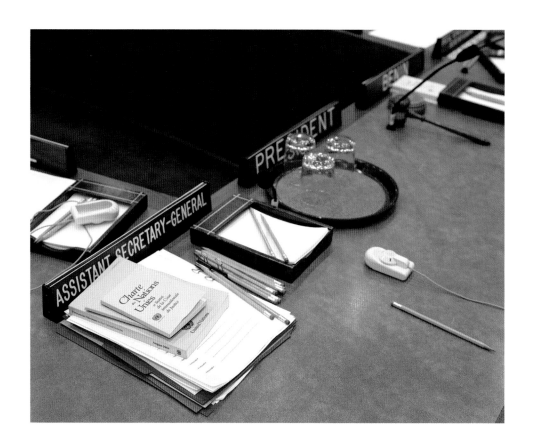

PAGES 110–113
In the Consultation Room, where the Security Council holds
informal meetings, the media and public are not allowed. Like the
main chamber, the room includes a horseshoe-shaped table, six
interpretation booths for simultaneous translation in the official
languages, a control room, and a large roll-down screen. Members of
the Security Council also hold meetings, sometimes bilaterally, in the
smaller Caucus Room next door.

Between the Conference Building and the General Assembly Building is the Japanese Peace Bell Garden, a gift from the Peace Bell Committee and other contributors at the wish of the Japanese community, inaugurated in 2000. The bell itself was donated in 1952 by the United Nations Association of Japan. Cast from pennies collected from children of all member States, it is primarily decorative, and is rung only on the first day of spring and on 21 September to commemorate the International Day of Peace.

FOLLOWING PAGES
One of several curving walls in the Conference Building that echo the General Assembly Building's walls and roof—a reminder that, although the individual structures have very different characters, they were conceived as a whole.

SECRETARIAT

A building chaste, startling, fairylike in its cold austerity, a Snow Queen's palace, exhaling by night a green, moonlight splendor.

— LEWIS MUMFORD

The most impossible job in the world.

— TRYGVE LIE

In the lobby of the General Assembly Building, seven portraits—silk rugs, given by the Islamic Republic of Iran in 1997—commemorate the seven Secretary-Generals who have held office since the United Nations was founded in 1945. From left, they are: Trygve Lie, of Norway (1946–52), who was involved in building the Headquarters; Dag Hammarskjöld, of Sweden (1953–61); U Thant, of Burma (now Myanmar, 1961–71); Kurt Waldheim, of Austria (1972–81); Javier Pérez de Cuéllar, of Peru (1982–91); Boutros Boutros-Ghali, of Egypt (1992–96); and Kofi Annan, of Ghana(1997–).

Koli ANNAN 1996

On the 38th floor of the Secretariat is the Secretary-General's suite of rooms. Over the years it has shown many faces (see page 29). As it appeared in 2003, when these photographs were taken (it has since been redecorated), it was a gift of the Austrian Chamber of Commerce during Kurt Waldheim's leadership. The conference room (RIGHT, AND FOLLOWING PAGE), decorated by Viennese architects Mr and Mrs Karl Mang and New York architect Gerhard Karplus, featured walnut paneling.

The Secretary-General's conference room featured an Austrian walnut table by Bernhard Ludwig, chairs by Taibel, and a Beauvais tapestry, *Le Ciel*, after Henri Matisse's painting (on loan from France since 1965). On the wall at left is *Landscape*, a watercolour by Raoul Dufy donated by UNICEF in 1979.

The Secretary-General's office overlooks the East River. The crystal
light fixtures here and in the private dining room (PAGE 127) are
from Lobmeyer of Vienna; the sofa and chairs are by Wittmann.
Despite changes to the office and conference room over the years,
the kitchen (FOLLOWING PAGE) remains largely as it was originally
installed.

ABOVE
Accessible from the Secretariat is the 750-seat cafeteria for staff
and delegates in the South Annex, a two-story building at the
south-east corner of the complex overlooking the East River,
completed in 1982. This view shows it prior to its renovation in
December 2004.

OPPOSITE
Midtown Manhattan seen from the Secretariat at dusk.

FOLLOWING PAGES
Among the prime spaces in the Secretariat are the women's
restrooms, looking across midtown Manhattan. At the time the
Secretariat was designed, the architects considered the view east
over the river more desirable, and therefore located the restrooms
on the western side. Extremely spacious and including a lounge,
they have glorious views of the skyline and the iconic Chrysler
Building, almost a stone's throw away. When the building is
renovated, such facilities will likely be moved to windowless
spaces at the center of each floor.

Some offices at the United Nations, such as these in the Secretariat, remain as they were originally designed. The two photographs show the typical layout and decoration of the office suite of a high-ranking official—in this case, an Under-Secretary-General. The office (ABOVE) gives directly on to a wood-paneled conference room (OPPOSITE). During the expected renovation of the Secretariat, the wood-paneled suites will be preserved as much as possible, though changes to the floor plans may mean that furnishings will be removed (and re-used).

The mail chutes (seen in the wall ABOVE) are still in operation
throughout the Secretariat.

There are 2 million square feet of flooring to be swept daily, and nearly 7 miles of carpeting for the vacuum cleaner. As pointed out in a caption to a photograph taken in 1953, originally the care of the corridors was not as straightforward as one might expect: "The beautiful floor of the Secretariat Building lobby—big black and white checks of terrazzo (made of marble chips)—presents a particular problem. The best way to polish this floor, according to chief Engineering Office, is for people to walk on it. However,

despite the steady stream of people, they walk in set paths across it. A sheen has to be produced artificially to avoid a contrast between the 'paths' and untrespassed areas. So the floor is washed nightly with a solution containing 30 per cent pure white soap, part of which remains and builds up a sheen. The floors at all the entrance ways of the Headquarters, as well as corridors near the elevator banks, are of terrazzo and receive the same special floor treatment."

The United Nations is a rich storehouse of information and knowledge and an active disseminator of humanitarian material. Aided by a twenty-four-hour printing press, the organization releases a significant number of publications and periodicals on its activities. In one year alone, it can generate some 50,000 documents, hundreds of publications in the six official languages (and occasionally in German), color posters and brochures. The printing facility, completed in 1981, is the largest internal reproduction plant in New York City and employs eighty-five people.

Approximately 1,400 tons of paper are collected each year under the
U.N. Paper Recycling Programme.

The Mail Operations Unit, which comprises mail, messengers and diplomatic pouches, employs about seventy-five people—ninety in the autumn, when the General Assembly is in session. The U.N. receives an average of 6.6 million pieces of mail per year, mostly from the United States. Worldwide, the office sends out some 600,000 pieces per year, and 1.2 million pounds of pouches to 187 overseas offices and missions.

There exist treasures of mid-20th-century design throughout the complex. The wayfinding signage, for example, features a sans-serif typeface (based on Futura) designed specially for the United Nations. In the Conference Building, curvilinear fixed seating and floor lights convey a sense of flight and provide a sculptural counterpoint to the rectilinear offices and corridors.

DAG HAMMARSKJÖLD LIBRARY

The underlying reason for the existence of the United Nations transcends both the circumstances of its creation and world political developments since that time. The reason is the interdependence of the world in which we live. We could not escape it if we wanted to.

— DAG HAMMARSKJÖLD

The Dag Hammarskjöld Library, connected to the Secretariat, was the fourth building in the U.N. Headquarters, dedicated in 1961 (some ten years after the complex's three original buildings were complete) to the memory of the second Secretary-General of the U.N., who was killed in a plane crash in Africa that same year. Designed by Harrison & Abramovitz and made possible by a gift from the Ford Foundation, the six-story building is constructed of white marble, glass and aluminum and houses the collections of the United Nations, specialized agencies and the League of Nations, general reference materials, and an extensive map collection.

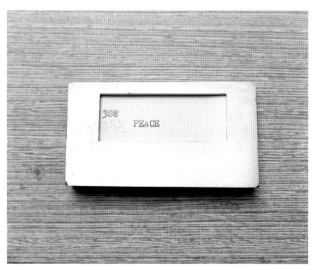

The Library contains approximately 400,000 volumes in its general collection and several million United Nations documents, along with newspapers, periodicals and maps on subjects of concern to the organization, such as the history of the U.N., political science, international relations, international and national law, disarmament, energy, economics, transport and communications, geography and social development. Its centerpiece is the Woodrow Wilson Reading Room, with a dramatic undulating white-pine ceiling.

FOLLOWING PAGES
The map section contains more than 80,000 maps and 1,500 atlases.

The Dag Hammarskjöld Auditorium, located in the Library's basement, was renovated in 2002 with funds offered by an undisclosed donor.

The 7-foot Steinway grand piano was presented to the United Nations in September 1985 in honor of the organization's fortieth anniversary by the National Federation of Music Clubs, a non-governmental organization in the United States, with funds from forty music clubs and more than one hundred individual donors.

The 184-seat auditorium is used for events that include recitals and concerts by the United Nations Singers, who perform in national dress.

FOLLOWING PAGES
The western wall of the penthouse in the Library is veneered in impressive hexagonal panels of English sycamore. The floor is bordered by Suprema Arabescato Fiorenzo marble. No longer furnished, the penthouse is used for formal receptions and for Muslim Friday prayers.

Looking east from 43rd Street toward the Secretariat (Tudor
City overlook).

The site of the United Nations is an international territory open to
the public in selected areas. Multi-language tours started as early
as November 1952 and over 38 million visitors have come to the U.N.
Building since its opening.

We are going to inscribe in stone and steel the achievements of the human race up to this time. In this way we can contribute toward the great objective to which we aspire all the time— the abolition of war.

— WARREN R. AUSTIN,
Permanent United States Delegate, 1947

A GLIMPSE OF THE FUTURE. The 2004 renovation of the GA 200 in the General Assembly Building is a gift to the United Nations from Switzerland, which became a Member in 2003. The impossibility of repairing the World Clock in the original GA 200 (page 53) is one of the reasons leading to the renovation of this vast space. A group of Swiss architects and artists, Inlay, won a national competition with a flexible plan of sliding walnut-veneered and red plate-glass partitions that allow for expansion and fluid movement. The word "peace" in the six official languages is inscribed in precious materials (gold, diamond, silver) and rare woods.